MUSEUMS & GALLERIES
COMMISSION

MUSEUMS MATTER

MUSEUMS & GALLERIES COMMISSION
16 Queen Anne's Gate, London SW1H 9AA
Telephone 071-233 4200 · Facsimile 071–233 3686

Registered Charity no. 295943

Museums & Galleries Commission

MUSEUMS MATTER

To:

The Right Honourable David Mellor, QC, MP, Secretary of State for National Heritage

The Right Honourable David Hunt, MBE, MP, Secretary of State for Wales

The Right Honourable Ian Lang MP, Secretary of State for Scotland

The Right Honourable Sir Patrick Mayhew, QC, MP, Secretary of State for Northern Ireland

On behalf of the Museums & Galleries Commission I have the honour to submit Museums Matter.

Graham Greene, *Chairman*

Peter Longman, *Director*

16 Queen Anne's Gate, 7 September 1992

Commissioners

Graham Greene Esq CBE
(Chairman)

The Marchioness of Anglesey DBE
(Vice-Chairman)

Dr Frank Atkinson OBE

The Baroness Brigstocke

Frederick Dunning Esq OBE

Professor Sir John Hale

Professor John Last CBE

Sir Hugh Leggatt

Professor David Michie RSA RGI FRSA

The Lord O'Neill TD DL

The Right Honourable The Lord Rees QC

Robert Smith Esq

Dame Margaret Weston DBE

Admiral Sir David Williams GCB DL

Contents

Two 1955 works, Balthus' 'Le Lever' and Richier's 'The Runner' face one another at the Scottish National Gallery of Modern Art, part of the National Galleries of Scotland. The Gallery complements its own outstanding collections with an exciting temporary exhibitions programme. Excellent use is made of limited purchase funds to make major acquisitions, which recently have included masterpieces by Miró and Moore.

Museums matter. A young visitor to the Ulster Folk & Transport Museum learns about, and is drawn into, the story of the 'Titanic'.

Foreword

GRAHAM GREENE
Chairman, Museums & Galleries Commission

Museums are among the most popular and successful faces of our artistic and cultural heritage. They are storehouses of knowledge – about the world we live in, its story and mankind's own progress, from the dawn of civilisation to the dawning of the 21st century. Their scope, and their appeal, are truly universal.

Museums have changed a good deal in the last twenty years. New methods of interpretation and display, and exciting new programmes and services, have all helped dispel the old fusty image. Less apparent to the public are the radical changes that have taken place in museum management. Museums have had to seek a balance between responding to social change and growing financial pressures, whilst not sacrificing traditional standards and duties. They are now much better placed to cater for fast-growing public interest in our environment, and our heritage.

This booklet is about museums in the United Kingdom, what they do, and why they are important to us all. It seeks to increase recognition of the remarkable number of ways in which they contribute to our society – as invaluable educational resources, centres for knowledge and research, generators of economic wealth, and ever more popular places for recreation and enjoyment.

I believe museums will have an even greater part to play, as we approach the Millenium. So we also here point the way forward, to what needs to be done to meet this challenge. We identify three main priorities: **to know what is in our collections, to care for and house them properly, and judiciously to add to them.**

These aims can be best achieved through genuine partnership – between central and local government, industry, individuals at every level and, not least, museums themselves. They will of course cost money, for which the new National Lottery is likely to be an essential source. We hope above all to have shown here that extra investment in museums more than pays for itself in many different ways.

The MGC has for over 60 years used its position at the centre of the museums world to advise and to influence developments. Together with our Area Museum Council partners, we shall during the coming years be working even harder to ensure the success story of museums in the UK is recognised, and that they are given the means to achieve their fullest potential.

Museums regularly feature among the country's top visitor attractions. Some 74 million visitors every year make museum visiting one of the most popular ways for people to spend free time. For many museums admission figures are still growing fast – at the Tate Gallery, where a changing programme of displays has excited lively public interest, admissions were up 14% in 1990 and, at 2.4 million, a further 10% in 1991.

Introduction – Museums and the MGC 1

The last 30 years have seen a transformation in the number and quality of our museums.* There are now well over 2000 compared with under 900 in 1962 and a new one appears to open every two weeks. The old fusty dusty image has largely been shaken off. Museums nowadays are exciting places to visit, lively treasure houses full of interest to connoisseur and curious alike. Their standards of display and visitor care have improved beyond recognition.

Good museums are indeed popular. They have a universal appeal, enabling people to see the roots of society and the culture they have inherited. By explaining history, and the rationale behind the physical and scientific world, museums help millions of people to understand life better and enjoy it more. In fact more people go to museums each year than go to football matches and the theatre combined – some 74 million in 1990. The UK's £7 billion overseas tourist industry needs museums for, with historic sites, they are the third most important factor in motivating people to visit this country; 27% of overseas visitors mention museums and galleries as a reason for visiting Britain.[1] But most museum visitors are British. In almost any city, town or village the museum is an important focus, a centre of the community, a reflection of civic pride and a sign of self-respect, a place for refreshment and enjoyment, a place of potential delight. Recent research by the Arts Council indicated that 32% of the adult population claimed to visit museums, a figure exceeded only by the 33% quoted for stately homes and the 45% for cinema among the cultural events listed.[2]

Museums have benefited from the recent increase in public awareness of heritage and conservation issues. Today they are rarely out of the news. Often

*Throughout this document the word "museum" may be taken to subsume "gallery".

it is a success story such as the Royal opening of a new building paid for by a generous benefactor, a new exhibition of a popular artist's work or an unexpected increase in government grant. Sometimes though it is a story of crisis: problems of building maintenance, the loss of a heritage item abroad, or the threat of staff cuts and closures.

The quality of a museum's collections enables it to combine education with delight as two sides of a single coin, for a good museum instructs in an enjoyable way. Museums are a major educational resource heavily used by teachers and school children. They are important too, for local history and planning, serving in effect as an information bank or three dimensional archive.

A museum's users are its customers. In the case of national and local authority museums the public are also the *owners,* whilst for independent museums, the paying public are the means of survival. So, museums exist to serve the public. This fact is reflected in the official definition that a museum is "an institution which collects, documents, preserves, exhibits and interprets material evidence and associated information for the public benefit".

As the definition also emphasises, it is the fact that a museum has a collection of original material that distinguishes it from most heritage and exhibition centres and theme parks. A museum is judged by its collections and by the use it makes of them in terms of care, research, display and access. The duty of long term care is fundamental, embracing not only the duty to care for and conserve, but also the duty to hold in trust for future generations. That is why a museum needs to have an institutional basis and why collections owned by private individuals are excluded.

For sixty years the Museums & Galleries Commission (MGC) has been the Government's main adviser on museum matters. Operating under a Royal Charter granted in 1987, we are funded by the Government but are independent of it. Our Chairman and fourteen Commissioners, all unpaid, are appointed by the Prime Minister. We are supported by a small professional staff. Together we have a strategic overview of the whole museum scene, covering all categories of museums (and non-commercial art galleries) and the whole of the UK. We are, in a strict sense, disinterested, and our advice is impartial. No other body concerned with museums has this combination of range, independence and impartiality.

In some ways the MGC is the counterpart of the Arts Council. Our concern for museums matches their's for the performing and creative arts, but we do not – and do not aspire to – fund the generality of museums on a revenue basis. We have an annual budget of about £9m, from which our main priority is to fund a limited number of organisations which work with us to provide support and services for museums individually and for the museum community as a whole. Although in the last ten years we have acquired a number of executive tasks, our most important role is still advisory and standard-setting, and our grants are mostly pump-priming and linked to the development and raising of standards.

It is from this standpoint that, in this booklet, we briefly survey the UK museum scene, note its main features and some of its problems, rehearse issues to be confronted and choices to be made. Our final chapter points to the future and makes some recommendations. In essence this booklet is an introduction for those who may not have time to read more, or who simply wish to pick up something of the flavour of current thinking in the museum community. Those who wish to follow up particular topics will find appropriate references and further information in the appendix.

Face to face across the millenia. A visitor to the National Museum of Wales in Cardiff admires the skeleton of an Edmontosaurus dinosaur on display in the Museum's Main Hall. The Edmontosaurus, which roamed modern South Dakota over 65 million years ago, is displayed along with even older dinosaur footprints from Bendricks near Barry. The National Museum's extremely diverse collections, which range from natural history to the fine arts, seek where possible to present the Principality's natural and artistic heritage in their wider international context.

The Museum Scene 2

Museum statistics are always complicated by the diversity of the museums themselves. Not only do museums come in all shapes and sizes and with different types of collection, but they are funded and organised in quite different ways. This means that statistics are assembled differently and are inconsistent. There are well over 2,000 places calling themselves 'museums' in the UK. If the definition is widened there may be as many as 2,500. Nobody knows exactly at present, but when the MGC's national registration scheme is complete we shall be able to say how many there are whose claims to fulfil the minimum standards expected are justified. This is not a function of size, because a respectable museum that meets these standards can be of the age and size and repute of the British Museum, or the smallest and newest village museum run by volunteers and open only at weekends.

The Government

There is no declared general Government policy on museums. Nor is there legislation applying to all museums, although some are covered by specific legislation.

The main responsibility for funding museums is shared between five Government Departments: the new Department of National Heritage (DNH) which took over the functions of the old Office of Art and Libraries in April 1992, the Ministry of Defence, and the Scottish, Welsh and Northern Ireland Offices. The DNH is the designated lead Department, but several other Departments have some regular involvement with museums, including notably the Department for Education which indirectly supports University museums, and the Department of the Environment in its dealings with local authorities.

National Museums

There is no statutory definition of a national museum, but the 19 institutions generally recognised as such have four characteristics in common: their collections are of national importance in terms of the United Kingdom or a part of it; they are vested in Trustees on the nation's behalf; they are wholly or mainly funded directly by Government; and the Government is able to call on their staff from time to time for such expert advice in their field as it may require.

Thirteen of the nationals are based in London, two in Edinburgh, one in Cardiff and two in Belfast. The British Museum (founded in 1753) is the oldest and largest. It heads the 'big six' London nationals, the others being the Victoria and Albert Museum, the National Gallery, the Tate Gallery, the Science Museum and the Natural History Museum. The National Museums and Galleries on Merseyside, a grouping of seven museums around Liverpool, were classed as a national museum only in 1986 following the abolition of the Merseyside County Council. Most of the national museums have branches outside the capital cities or operate from several sites. The National Museum of Wales, for example, has eleven branches. And the Science Museum, as the National Museum of Science and Industry, operates also the National Railway Museum in York and the National Museum of Photography, Film and Television in Bradford. Between them the national museums have some 50 branch museums or outstations, attract 25 million visitors a year and employ over 6,000 staff – nearly one-third of all paid staff working in UK museums. In 1991–92 they received some £232m in grants-in-aid from central government, of which some 62% was for running costs, 33% for building and maintenance, and 5% for acquisitions. Together the national museums generate some £52m each year from fund raising and sponsorship, trading and admission charges and donations.

Every one of the national museums has all or most of its Trustees (or equivalents) appointed by the Government, which provides them with an annual grant-in-aid and expects them to be responsible for the well-being of their collections and the buildings which house them. This is commonly spoken of as the 'arm's length' principle. The length of the arm can vary. The freedom of the Trustees and their quasi-independence from Government doubtless have their advantages, but these are inherently difficult to reconcile with factors such as the Trustees not having effective control over their salary bills (pay awards are determined between the Government and the Civil Service Unions), not being provided with enough money to pay their staff salaries or discharge their responsibilities of collection care properly, and not being able to borrow money. The system works reasonably well up to a point, but it rests on too uneasy a balance of power and responsibility to be really satisfactory, and some Trustees feel that they have insufficient information to make important decisions.

A number of other museums receive all or most of their funding direct from the Government. These include the Sir John Soane's Museum and the Horniman and Geffrye Museums in London (DNH), and the Ulster American Folk Park (Department of Education for Northern Ireland). The DNH also funds the Museum of Science and Industry in Manchester and (jointly with the City of London) the Museum of London, and (through the MGC) part of the costs of the Tyne and Wear Museum Service.

University Museums

The first museum to be opened to the public (nearly 70 years before the British Museum) was the Ashmolean Museum in Oxford, the oldest of some 300 university museums and collections throughout the UK. They are mainly funded from government money which universities receive from the Education Departments through the Universities Funding Council (UFC), and they range from large and famous institutions open to the public to small departmental collections used only for teaching purposes or not at all. A few of these museums receive help from or have been taken over by local authorities. Museums in this sector probably face greater problems than any others, as the funding for universities is under growing pressure, and is likely to be further reviewed from 1993. The UFC grants to 15 universities currently include an element of Special Factor funding in respect of 25 of the more important museums or collections. This system should be refined and extended, but there are fears that it may be stopped.

Armed Services Museums

A third category of museums, also mainly or partly funded by central government, is that of the 200 or so museums of the armed services. Those directly or indirectly under the aegis of the Ministry of Defence range from the national museums of the Army and the Royal Air Force, and those of the Royal Navy, to well over 100 smaller regimental and corps museums and collections, many of them based in regimental headquarters, and many operating on a bare minimum of part-time or voluntary staff. These too are under increasing pressure resulting from defence cuts and the fact that the MOD (although it is currently reviewing its policy) does not see museums as central to the role of the armed services.

Local Authority Museums

If the national museums form the hub of the UK museum system, local authority museums are the spokes of the wheel. Most District and many County Councils operate some form of museum service. Many were founded in the 19th century and a high proportion are based in listed buildings. The total number has increased in recent years and, including branch museums, is now around 800. Expenditure by local authorities was around £128m in 1991–92, of which around £100m was covered by the government's block grant. Some 25 million visitors are attracted annually.

Local authority museums vary greatly in size, quality and importance. Glasgow City Museums Service, which includes the Burrell Collection and Kelvingrove Museum as well as eight other sites, has an annual budget of £13.3m, employs 423 staff and receives some 2.5m visitors. These figures are unrivalled except by a handful of the largest national museums, and many other local authorities spend in excess of £1m annually. Collections like those of the Bowes Museum, now funded by Durham County Council, rival those of many national museums. At the other end of the scale, some local authority museums comprise no more than one room in a library run by a part-time member of staff. Many play an important role as interpreters of local history, and as biological, geological and archaeological record centres. What they all maintain in common is a long-standing commitment to local education and community service.

Generally local authority museums are run as part of a larger department. In the past this was usually education or libraries, but today museums are more likely to come under the wing of leisure services, or tourism or even economic development. Although some local authority museums still deserve the unfortunate epithet of "worthy but dull", and they generally have a traditional feeling and appearance, great improvements have been made in management and presentation in recent years. Some of the most striking recent developments have taken place in Northern Ireland at places like Derry and Downpatrick and often with the help of capital funding from outside agencies. But standards and practice do vary widely. Much depends on the calibre and interest of those involved at officer and elected member level, and on how the local authority concerned has been affected by the recent changes in legislation and local government finance. The government block grants to local authorities take no account of their museum responsibilities, which are often regional or national rather than purely local, and many museums face further threats with the possible disappearance of County Councils and continued moves towards contracting out management of local authority services to the private sector.

Independent Museums

The most numerous are the independent museums, which number upwards of 1100. Nearly all are set up as charitable trusts, and most receive no regular funding from central or local government. The best are characterised by innovation, by creative flair and energy, and by awareness of the needs of their visitors, on whom nearly all depend financially for survival. Frequently this is supplemented by a significant voluntary input, for such museums tend to be started by enthusiastic individuals or groups. Not surprisingly, this has been the fastest-growing sector, but it is now the most vulnerable to changes in the national economy, and at risk from competition from other types of visitor attraction. Fewer new ones are being created, whilst an increasing number each year languish and are forced to close. So far this has mainly affected privately owned institutions run for profit and thus outside the scope of this booklet, but the trend is unmistakable.

Support for Museums

The Government's main direct input is through its sponsorship of the 19 nationals. It also funds the *Museums & Galleries Commission* (MGC), which is the Government's official advisory body for museums of all types throughout the UK and has direct contacts with each of the departments concerned. The MGC is also in regular contact with museums and has published or commissioned reports on each of the museum sectors outlined above, as well as on particular parts of the UK and on specific subjects such as training. However, the usual channel of support for non-national museums and galleries is at a regional level through the *Area Museum Councils* (AMCs). These were set up by and are run by museum interests on a membership basis. They employ professional staff to advise museums, and some provide specialist services, such as conservation or travelling exhibitions. They also make small grants for "one-off" projects, help co-ordinate the provision of training, and provide an essential first port of call for anyone wishing to start a new museum or redevelop an existing one. The MGC funds the seven English AMCs, the Scottish Office Education Department funds the Scottish Museums Council, and the Welsh Office the Council of Museums in Wales. The Department of Education for Northern Ireland helps to fund the Northern Ireland Museums Advisory Committee – from which, it is hoped, an AMC for Northern Ireland will emerge.

The work of the AMCs is co-ordinated by the Committee of AMCs (CAMC), and by means of regular meetings between AMC Chairmen and Directors with the MGC and its staff. Although the AMCs are independently run, in practice they work very closely with us, particularly on the museum registration scheme and in assessing grant applications. The system works well, though far more money is needed. The nine AMCs receive less than £4m in total, a figure that should be at least doubled if they are fully to exploit their potential in assisting and improving museums and museum services.

The museum profession is a small one and fragmented. There is relatively little movement between different types of museum, and this is exacerbated by different pay and grading scales. Many small museums and some larger ones rely very heavily on volunteers. About one-third of the total workforce of 25,000 is in this category. Salary levels outside the nationals are generally low. Those working in independent museums are often in their second career whilst others, especially in University and Armed Service museums, find themselves combining museum duties with other roles. Only the larger museums are able to employ specialists in such areas as administration, marketing or design. A high proportion of all staff are engaged in warding and security. Curators – people trained to understand and look after collections – are frequently in the minority and often find themselves having to undertake many other tasks as well. Only in the national museums and in others which have more specialised collections are curators likely to be able to concentrate on their special subjects.

The *Museum Training Institute* was established in 1989 as a direct result of the MGC's report on training and career structure,[3] and in response to Government legislation intended to produce a trained workforce by the year 2000. It is now funded by the DNH, and has the support of the Department of Employment and the National Council for Vocational Qualifications in its important task of overseeing and co-ordinating the provision of training for those who work in museums, of developing standards of competence in each functional area, and of maximising the involvement of museum staff and their employers in training initiatives.

The other support organisation mainly funded by the Government (through the MGC) is the *Museum Documentation Association.* This works to raise standards of documentation in museums and to encourage and help them to document their collections more comprehensively and consistently, especially with the use of computers.

The main professional organisation of museums and their staff is the *Museums Association,* the first such body to be set up in the world and now into its second century. Although its fortunes have fluctuated through the years, it has done pioneering work on in-service training and offers a widely recognised professional qualification, an annual conference and the monthly Museums Journal. Most of its members come from the local authority sector, but its Museums Yearbook contains codes of practice, policy statements and guidelines for the whole museum community. Each region has a *Federation of Museums and Art Galleries* run on a voluntary basis and affiliated to the Association, and there is also a bewilderingly large number of *Specialist Groups and Societies,* covering different subjects or specific areas of activity. With a membership of 800 institutions, the *Association of Independent Museums* (AIM) is particularly influential. It produces the AIM Bulletin every other month and an excellent series of Guidelines on aspects of museum management, and also organises training seminars.

Well over 200 museums have their own organisation of *Friends* of the museum; some 150,000 people are involved, many of whom work as volunteers or help with fundraising. Their umbrella organisation is the *British Association of Friends of Museums* (BAFM).

The main *international organisation* is the International Council of Museums (ICOM), with headquarters in Paris. UK museum staff are active in its work and in that of its specialist committees, such as conservation, training and security. The UK also contributes (through the MGC and others) to the International Centre for the Study of the Preservation and Restoration of Cultural Property (ICCROM), with headquarters in Rome. Until recently there was no established museums forum within Europe but one is now being set up.

The main *charities supporting museums* include the National Art Collections Fund (NACF), which makes grants to museums totalling some £1.5m a year to help them with specific purchases. It publishes an Art Quarterly and an Annual Review, and runs an annual awards scheme. The Contemporary Arts Society, also a membership body, buys new works from artists and presents them to museums. The main pressure group and lobby, the National Campaign for the Arts, publishes occasional leaflets in support of museums, but is mainly concerned with the performing arts organisations and their funding. On a more limited scale National Heritage has given support to museums over the years and runs the prestigious 'Museum of the Year Award' scheme.

A number of charitable trusts including those associated with the names of Carnegie, Wolfson, Leverhulme and Pilgrim have been generous over many years in giving grants to museums for particular projects.

Finally, mention should be made of the *National Heritage Memorial Fund,* set up in 1980 under Trustees and funded by the Government. It has a good record of helping museums, national and non-national, to acquire and conserve works for which their own purchase grants were insufficient, but its terms of reference also include the built and the natural environment.

Cheltenham Art Gallery and Museum is a leading local authority museum. Its collections, of great diversity and quality, include an internationally important collection of Arts and Crafts furniture and decorative arts. These have recently been redisplayed in a new extension, part of a redevelopment programme funded by the local authority. However, funding for running costs and staffing, a traditional problem for local authority museums, is now being exacerbated by cutbacks in local authority education spending.

A student compares drawings by the Venetian renaissance masters Bellini and Carpaccio in the Printroom of the Ashmolean Museum. The Ashmolean houses one of the world's greatest collections of prints and drawings, including unrivalled groups of drawings by artists as diverse as Pissarro and Raphael, making it a mecca for scholars and researchers. But the Museum welcomes all visitors to the Printroom, which is open to the public six days a week.

Research and Scholarship 3

If a museum's collections are to be properly used it is essential first to know and understand them. It is in the nature of museums that, where there is a collection and a curator, there is an opportunity – and a need – for scholarship. From whatever background they come and on whatever basis they are engaged, true museum people are motivated first and foremost by their concern for objects. A museum's scholarly approach, inculcated by its traditions and by its director, should dictate and inform all its work. Scholarship and research should underpin every form of museum activity. Conservation relies upon it, interpretation and display derive from it, and educational services need it as a foundation.

World class research is carried out in our scientific museums, using their unrivalled collections. Taxonomic (classification) work and biological studies are helping the world to defeat a variety of tropical diseases, and support all kinds of agricultural and health programmes. The Natural History Museum's research programmes directly benefit the international community and especially the people of the third world. The concern expressed when the museum's 1990 corporate plan proposed cutbacks in some areas and changes in its priorities for research came not only from other museums but from the scientific community around the world.

British archaeology is another area where the learning and experience of our museums has long led the way for other countries better to understand and preserve their own cultural heritages. Our wealth of art collections and long tradition of teaching in art history have enabled Britain's museums to make substantial contributions to international art historical research and scholarship. The National Gallery's established series of collection catalogues set new standards in the presentation and discussion of detailed scholarly information.

Scholarship is not in any way confined to the large national museums. The display of more modest collections also needs a basis of scholarly research and interpretation. A good example – one of the many that could be cited – is the Weald and Downland Open Air Museum at Singleton in West Sussex, where research into historic building methods and materials precisely complements its displays and reconstructed buildings.

Scholarship does not need to be remote from the public. An exhibition series underlined this point: the National Gallery's "Art in the Making", which explained the technical process behind the creation of pictures, enjoyed unexpected success, attracting the public in large numbers. There is a receptive public evidently avid for knowledge and experience, and unwilling to be patronised, as well as a public looking for less in-depth entertainment with an educational dimension. Too often museums have yielded to the temptation to put on a popular exhibition or display simply in order to generate increased visitor numbers or to balance their budgets. Too often, scholarship is seen only in terms of a finite research or publication programme which can be cut or even dropped when money is short. A museum without a scholarly dimension is as much a contradiction in terms as one not open to the public.

The setting and maintenance of standards in scholarship and research are no less important than in other fields of museum work. A museum must be able to demonstrate – to its paymasters, to the public, to Parliament, as well as to itself and its own Trustees – that it is performing well as a museum and providing a qualitatively high level of visitor experience; that it has not lost its integrity and that it is maintaining its intellectual standards. These intellectual standards can in the first instance be self-generated. In our *Report 1989–90*[4] we said we should like to see each museum's corporate plan set out what the museum perceives is expected of it in terms of intellectual standards and of visitor attractions; how it has translated those perceptions into its objectives; and how far it has attained those objectives.

Ideally, of course, standards should be set objectively, and not simply subjectively. The objective assessment of quality is notoriously difficult, and expensive. In the United States, museums invest heavily in assessment programmes: their accreditation process involves peer-group reviews and a self-study lasting a year. In the UK, an accreditation system on the US model was tried by the Museums Association some years ago and abandoned as too expensive. We do not advocate the general adoption of such a system, though it is no doubt an ideal at which the museum community should be aiming.

Dr Darrell Siebert of The Natural History Museum's Biodiversity Programme alongside a few of the million or so specimens in the Museum's fish collection. With over 67 million objects the Museum is the largest of its type in the world. Its collections are a unique storehouse of knowledge, which are at the base of the Museum's international reputation as a centre for taxonomic research.

Conservator Ellen Breheny works on a relief of the Madonna and Child, a 19th century plaster cast after an original marble by the 15th century sculptor Domenico Rosselli, in preparation for its inclusion in a new permanent display at the Royal Museum of Scotland in Edinburgh. UK museums have contributed significantly to advances in scientific knowledge of techniques and materials, which have transformed conservation techniques during the past two decades. Nevertheless, good conservation ultimately will always depend on the patience and skill of highly-trained individuals.

Caring for Collections 4

Since it is their collections of original material that distinguish museums from an exhibition centre or an artificial theme park, and which give museums their unique appeal, clearly it is the prime duty of a museum to care for those collections. The term collection-care (or collection management) takes in the whole range of museum activity: research and documentation, ensuring that any necessary conservation work is undertaken, and that there are proper conditions for storage and display including physical security and environmental monitoring and control.

A century or more of curatorial experience has enabled the museum community to accumulate a vast body of knowledge about general and specific aspects of collection-care, and to develop a broad consensus about how different sorts of collections should be documented, preserved, housed and stored. Much of the received wisdom in relation to particular specialisms is reflected in the work of the various Specialist Groups that operate under the aegis of the Museums Association. And much of it is distilled in the Manual of Curatorship which, published under the Association's auspices, first appeared in 1984.[5]

A report published for the Museums Association and the Office of Arts and Libraries in 1989[6] on the Cost of Collecting drew attention to the financial implications – showing that for many classes of item the costs of acquisition were minimal in comparison with the true subsequent costs of looking after them. The Public Accounts Committee also drew attention to the backlogs of work in documentation and conservation following an examination of some of the London based national institutions,[7] and a recent Audit Commission report[8] has also drawn attention to the same problems as they exist in local authority museums. Such reports echo things that the museum profession has been saying for many years, but it is encouraging to know that government, both central and local, now appreciates that expenditure behind the scenes is just as essential and important as creating new displays and public facilities. For most museums the collections on display are usually the tip of the iceberg. Apart from lack of display space, there are sound reasons for this situation. Sensitive material such as watercolours or textiles cannot be placed on continuous public display without irreparable damage, while the majority of items from an archaeological excavation, for example, do not lend themselves to public display and are more usefully kept in store as a study collection. Nevertheless, as far as possible, the best objects are usually displayed.

In the last few years the MGC and the Area Museum Councils have perceived the need for a comprehensive series of standards, covering all aspects of museum work, and these are now being evolved. By 1989 we had committed ourselves to the central aim of setting and improving standards in UK museums. There was of course evident room for improvement, but we started from the basis that no one knew how high – or low – museum standards were, because there were no standards. Moreover, no one knew how many museums there were, or what were the minimum requirements for a museum.

The first need therefore was a national registration scheme for museums. This the MGC had launched in 1988 with a programme of initial registration, phased by AMC areas over four years, which will be completed in 1992. Guidelines based largely on the Museums Association's Codes of Practice were agreed with the museum community. The main requirements of registration are that a museum should have an appropriate constitution and sound financial basis, an agreed collecting policy and proper standards of collections management, appropriate public opening hours and facilities, and access to professional curatorial advice. The Area Museum Councils act as the MGC's agents in the registration process, helping museums with their applications and advising the MGC. So far over 1300 museums have been registered, ranging from the British Museum to a small one-room establishment run on a voluntary basis. In essence Registration is a seal of approval for the benefit of visitors and users, potential benefactors and other government agencies and local authorities. It has the backing of the Local Authority Associations, the Audit Commission, and the

Cathedral in iron and glass: the magnificent Main Hall of the Royal Museum of Scotland, designed by Captain Francis Fowke RE *in 1861. The Hall houses a variety of displays, as well as the Museum's information desk and its shop. Not least, its fountains and light-filled spaces make a relaxing and popular place for visitors to rest from their 'museum feet'!*

Government as well as many other grant-giving bodies. A system of annual returns ensures that the information initially provided is up-to-date and still valid. This will provide the basis for an annual digest of museum statistics (DOMUS), for which a need has long been seen.

The registration guidelines are no more than a baseline of minimum common standards and objectives for all sizes and types of museums. But on this foundation the MGC is now developing a comprehensive series of standards and guidelines, by which museums can assess themselves and be assessed by their governing bodies and paymasters. Once these standards are set, a museum will not only have a clear incentive to do what is required to meet them; it will also have the means of making an objective case for any extra funds it may need to enable it to meet those standards.

A museum object can be useless without its associated information and unless its existence is properly recorded. The *documentation* of museum collections is an area that lends itself to standards development, especially in relation to new technology. Many museums have considerable backlogs in documenting their collections even manually, and to be eligible for registration they must demonstrate that they are taking effective steps to reduce these. The Museum Documentation Association (which the MGC largely funds) is working to develop a nationally agreed data standard or set of guidelines for recording information about objects in a consistent and effective way. The MDA offers a low cost documentation software package, MODES, which has given many museums the opportunity to computerise their documentation processes. In parallel a consortium of major museums, LASSI, is exploring with the MGC the feasibility of joint development of a new generation collections management system for use in larger museums.

Standards have already been set for museum *security* by the MGC's Museums Security Adviser, and these must be met before a government indemnity is issued in respect of a loan. Museums are also given advice when planning new buildings or extensions, or changes to their security arrangements.

Display and storage are also key areas for standards, which will vary for different types of collections. The MGC has already published standards for caring for archaeological material as the first in a series of such documents, and is now developing those for industrial material and natural sciences collections. Proper *environmental conditions and monitoring* is an important aspect of caring for objects. The MGC expects to be issuing guidelines on this towards the end of 1992. We hope that with time these will become the accepted approach to environmental control in museums.

The condition of museum buildings is of course a major factor in this context. Many are very important in their own right and many are old. Many others are ageing buildings of indifferent quality. Striking a balance between the claims of a fine historic building and the demands of the collections it houses is not always easy. Of far more fundamental concern is the fact that many of the buildings, particularly those of the nationals in London, have suffered years of neglect. The cost of restoring the nation's fabric of museum buildings and creating the additional facilities needed is likely to exceed £2,000m over a 10-year period. In recent years the government has increased greatly its contributions to restoring the 19 national museums, but much more still needs to be done for them, while the task of upgrading the other 2000 (over half of them listed buildings) will be a major claim on the proceeds of the proposed National Lottery.

In all these areas the MGC is taking the lead in developing *standards*. It is doing so with the full support of the museum community, including the Area Museum Councils, the Museums Association and the Association of Independent Museums. It is part of the museum community's response to the need to show it is providing value for money. It is also a response to the need for museums to be accountable for the care of the collections entrusted to them.

Getting to grips with bridge building: father and daughter explore together the technology behind bridges crossing over canals. One of many innovative hands-on educational displays at a leading independent museum, the National Waterways Museum in Gloucester.

Serving the Museum User 5

Studies have shown that, if persuaded across the threshold of a museum, most people find something to interest them and make a visit worthwhile. The challenge is not only to provide a good experience for those who do visit, but to improve marketing techniques in order to attract those who do not. A recent survey of non-visitors elicited the memorable description "dingy places with different kinds of bits"[9] but the visitor numbers and audience surveys indicate that museums do have a very broad appeal, and that all socio-economic groups are generally well represented. However it has to be admitted that As and Bs tend to predominate. The typical visitor is British and comes as part of a family group as a leisure activity with an educational slant. But many other sectors are heavily represented. In London and other popular tourist destinations, there are significant numbers of overseas visitors. However the attendance levels in areas with high Asian or Afro-Caribbean populations are often found to be disappointingly low, although there are increasing examples of better provision for these sectors by involving them in decisions about what sort of exhibitions and activities will be appreciated.

The unique selling point of a museum is the fact that it has collections and that the public is lured by the opportunity to see the 'real thing' rather than a replica or a reproduced image. The point has been made earlier that scholarship and the research it engenders should inform a museum's displays and exhibitions and determine the quality of its visitors' experience. Good interpretation is a function of scholarship, and the form it takes will vary of course with the nature of the display. Paintings, at one extreme, may need only a brief caption though this must be clear and authoritative. Scientific exhibits may well need animation and interaction to make them intelligible, but this must be reliable as well as authoritative. Sadly, standards of display and presentation in many museums are still appalling. Often it is not money or access to an experienced designer that is lacking, but imagination.

The technique and design of labels is a subject that has received some attention from museums, but probably not enough. A notable contribution was the National Maritime Museum's *The Writing on the Wall,* published in 1989. Questions of label-height, size of print and layout are clearly crucial. Yet too often there are exhibitions where the experience is marred by inconveniently placed labels with print too small for the visitor to read in the necessarily subdued lighting conditions. One wonders what thought the designer gave to the visitor's needs and expectations.

Here we may mention the needs of the museum visitor or staff with some disability or impairment: the partially-sighted, the deaf or partly deaf, the ill or elderly who cannot stand for long, those who find steps difficult, those with children in pushchairs and (only 2% of all those with a disability) the wheel-chair user. It can be difficult for museums to strike a sensible balance between the needs of different users, and many museum buildings are old and difficult to adapt. But the MGC will this year be issuing guidance to museums, stating the principles and outlining best practice.

The educational function of a museum has always been central to its purpose. It is implicit in almost all it does, and applies to visitors of all ages and academic backgrounds. Most museums give an explicit dimension to this function in the shape of the service they provide for schoolchildren. Museum education services now have a new prominence because of the introduction of the General Certificate of Secondary Education (GCSE) and the National Curriculum, with their emphasis on learning from original sources. In the context of the National Curriculum museums have a vast potential to offer; the MGC has written to governors of all maintained schools spelling out the educational opportunities that museums present to pupils and their teachers. We have recommended too that museums should develop educational policies and where possible employ specialist education staff – of their own or shared – and ideally funded by local authorities. Most regrettably, pressure on local education authority budgets and the devolution of additional financial responsibility to schools has resulted in cuts to many museum education services just when museums had most to offer.

One has only to go into a museum shop and see it crowded with children (and adults when there is room) to realise the close connection between school visits and the shop. Some museums operate a shop primarily for its educational and public relations value. Four museums out of five now have a shop or sales-point, and in many there is clearly scope for developing this as a money-making facility. Catering is another area where standards still vary greatly and where there are often opportunities for development.

Nowadays museums operate in a far more competitive environment than was the case 10 years ago. They must compete, in what they offer visitors, with what can be seen on television or experienced at the nearby theme park, and with the many other demands commonly made on leisure time, not least gardening and shopping. So museums have to be attractive in terms of the value they offer for the time and money expended on the visit, and in every aspect of what they offer. Museums must provide good family facilities; an imaginatively stocked shop; catering facilities; clean lavatories; baby changing facilities and a room for nursing mothers; good information and clear signposting. Nor must they ignore the most common complaint to afflict museum visitors – 'museum feet' – easily remedied with comfortable public seating. The Tourist Boards have recently agreed The National Code of Practice for Visitor Attractions. This has been welcomed by the museum community, for it complements the guidance already provided through the registration scheme and the customer care code which we will be issuing shortly. A museum should aspire to be as welcoming to the visitor in catering for physical needs and comforts as in providing for intellectual refreshment.

Patronage old and new at Britain's oldest public museum, the Ashmolean in Oxford, founded in 1683. The surviving nucleus of the celebrated Arundel Collection of ancient sculpture was given by Countess Pomfret to Oxford in 1755. Almost 250 years later, in 1991, a major gift from Dr and Mrs von Bothmer enabled the Ashmolean to refurbish the sculpture gallery to its original splendour.

Collecting and the Heritage 6

Britain is extraordinarily rich in its museums, and in the variety and depth of their collections. They range from the personal and idiosyncratic like Sir John Soane's Museum in London, a shrine reflecting its original owner's taste, to the wonderfully encyclopedic like the National Museum of Wales, bringing together treasures of all sorts from every stream of Welsh life and beyond in buildings scattered throughout the Principality; from a brilliant combination of original artefacts and carefully researched reproductions at the Jorvik Centre in York, to the remnants of a one-industry place like the Museum of Leadmining at Wanlockhead in Scotland's highest village. The distribution of museums, like the assembly of collections, owes much to circumstances and chance. Some subjects, such as church plate, or the railway age, are well covered in our museums. Others, such as icons, or postage stamps, are represented in only a few public collections. Some industries, such as the motor industry, have museums displaying their products, though not their manufacture. Some, such as steel or civil engineering, have little or nothing to show for themselves in museums. Urgent action is needed if a representative range of historic industrial machinery and industrial sites are to be preserved, particularly in Scotland where industry has played such an important role in the country's history.

Recording the present day for the museum visitors of the future is problematic for many museums. Excellence and significance are hard to select from the wealth of choice and on limited budgets. The lack of proper storage space and shortages of staff are further constraints. Many museums have so instilled into themselves the virtues of inalienability, the strength of the presumption against disposal, that they are wary of saddling themselves with unwanted, unrepresentative objects and the ever increasing costs of caring for them. This is a dilemma out of which museums must get themselves – through more flexible procedures for determining which material should be finally accepted into their collections, and by reassessing their existing holdings. The adoption of a formal collecting policy is a key requirement of the MGC's registration scheme. Museums of a similar kind should work together and concert their collecting policies. It may be appropriate for one of the national museums to take the lead, as the National Maritime Museum and the National Ships Preservation Committee have done in the case of historic ship preservation. For some types of collection, such as artillery, co-ordination on a national scale should be possible; for others, such as archaeology or social history, this is best done on a regional or even local basis.

A habit of concerting collecting policies should lead to a more consistent approach to existing collections. Many museums hold modest collections in subjects outside their main field of interest. In some fields (natural history is one) there are many more small collections in museums than there are trained curators to care for them. Some museums have a modest collection (a few stuffed animals, some geological specimens) which they can hardly display or interpret, and of which they would really rather be rid. It is in everyone's interest that in these instances arrangements should be made for the collection to be transferred (by gift or loan) to another museum which is willing to curate and display it, or by a joint arrangement to provide storage for what would be in effect a regional reserve collection of particular material. Such rationalisation should be encouraged and the appropriate major museums and Area Museum Councils could well give a lead.

Even after such rationalisations many museums will find themselves still in possession of material that is either outside their sphere of interest, duplicates existing holdings, or that has so deteriorated in condition as to be of no use or interest. In such circumstances recourse to sale or even destruction may well be appropriate. The procedures for such a course of action are laid down in the Museums Association Code of Practice for Museum Authorities and in the registration scheme guidelines, and in legislation for the nationals; museums should be able to follow them without provoking fears that this will encourage enforced sales of one-off items or works of art for financial gain. Sales for financial gain are, fortunately, very rare and are a betrayal of the trust in which museum collections are held. Let it never be forgotten that the majority of museum collections were not purchased but donated, and that a museum exists for the public benefit.

The ability of museums to collect contemporary material on a planned basis, and a willingness to rationalise existing collections in appropriate instances, are two aspects of reform the MGC would like to see. A third is equally important; the ability to acquire items for its collections is one of the hallmarks of a healthy museum. And yet purchase grants for the DNH-funded national museums have been frozen in cash terms since 1985. They urgently need to be at least doubled. More money also needs to be provided to the National Heritage Memorial Fund, and to the MGC and the National Museums of Scotland, which make purchase grants to non-national museums. No huge sums of money are needed: an additional £25m a year would transform the scene. Even then the prices commanded by such masterpieces as Holbein's Portrait of a Lady with a Squirrel and a Starling, the Three Graces, the Badminton Cabinet, and the Canaletto of Old Horse Guards in London would still present problems to museums wishing to acquire them through outright purchase at open market prices. At present too much reliance has to be placed on the generosity of private individuals.

There are a number of tax incentives designed to prevent private owners from having to sell important heritage items and to ensure that museums can acquire them in the event of a sale being necessary. An owner may apply for *conditional exemption* for an object that is of museum quality. As long as certain conditions are fulfilled the value of the object is not taken into account when calculating its owner's tax liabilities. Under the *acceptance-in-lieu* scheme the State is able to accept important objects in settlement of certain tax debts, and the objects are then transferred to the ownership of a museum. Under certain circumstances it is even possible for the object to be taken into public ownership and yet remain *in situ* in its original setting, provided there is reasonable public access. The effectiveness of acceptance-in-lieu has been greatly increased in recent years, but the tax incentive given to owners (the douceur) needs to be increased from 25% to 50%. Finally, owners and museums may both benefit by using the arrangements for *private treaty sales;* under this scheme a special low price is agreed between both parties because the tax that would otherwise have been payable on an open market sale has been avoided. Greater use can and should be made of all these incentives, but some further reforms are needed.

We believe that tax relief should also be allowed on gifts in kind to museums, as they are now allowed on gifts of cash. Such a scheme operates successfully in Australia and in the USA.

Taken together with increased funding and gift-aid in kind, these measures allow owners and executors to secure a better and surer return than they could expect to receive from sale by auction, while still affording the art-trade the opportunity to advise and negotiate on valuation on the owner's behalf. Negotiations would be undertaken in proper commercial confidence, rather than in the glare and trauma that attends an export-stop after an auction sale. The alternative, to draw up a list of pre-eminent items the export of which would be prohibited, has fortunately been rejected by the Government.

Export control after 1992 with reduced customs controls will at best be problematical, with the need to harmonise the UK arrangements with those of the rest of the European Community. The recent report of the Government's Export Reviewing Committee contained many excellent recommendations whereby the UK's system could be improved and serve as a model for others.

Its greatest strength is that it preserves a proper balance between the interests of private owners, the art trade, and museums. But if it is to work effectively, and if museums are to continue to acquire material for their collections, additional funding is needed now.

The Pitt Rivers Museum in Oxford has been justly called an 'Aladdin's cave of treasures'. Its genesis, the public-spirited gift by an eminent Victorian of the Museum's founding collection, is typical of many museums in Britain. Few have managed to maintain so successfully the appearance of organised clutter which for many sums up the charm of museums. But appearances can often be deceptive. The Pitt Rivers houses one of the world's great ethnographic collections and, despite severe funding problems, maintains extremely important research and education programmes.

The Fife Folk Museum in Ceres is housed in an outstanding group of 17th and 18th century buildings. Opened as recently as 1968, the Museum is one of hundreds in Britain established and largely run by volunteers. Such museums play a major role in their communities and are a great source of local pride. Many have become well-known in their own right and now attract large numbers of visitors from further afield in the UK and abroad, thereby contributing significantly to local economies.

Paying for Museums 7

Museums are a long-term investment, a resource held in trust by the present for future generations and that cannot be realised or liquidated. The care of their collections requires expenditure on staff and equipment that may bring no immediate return or tangible benefit, even though it has been shown[10] that the wider economic impact of the arts and museums is often considerable. So, almost inevitably, public museums – those established by central or local government – need public funding for their basic operations. In a report in 1988,[11] the MGC asserted that the Government has a clear responsibility to fund the essential activities of national museums. And in a report in early 1991[12] we urged that local authorities operating a museum should ensure that it has enough revenue to be able to comply with the MGC's registration guidelines.

The Government spent some £259m in 1991–92 on the direct funding of museums, of which most (some £232m) went to the nineteen national museums, divided between running costs, purchase grants and building costs.

Successive governments have always maintained that, with the exception of the nationals, museums were essentially a local responsibility. In this crucial regard the Government treats museums differently to the performing arts. In a typical provincial city the orchestra, repertory theatre or arts centre will receive substantial support each year towards its running costs through the Arts Council or Regional Arts Board, but the museum will be a wholly local responsibility, eligible only for occasional small one-off grants from the MGC or the local AMC for specific projects. Typically, AMC grants range from under £100 to £5–10,000 whilst those from the MGC are not much bigger.

Local authorities spent some £128m on museums in 1991–92 (£106m in England, £13m in Scotland, £7m in Wales, £1m in Northern Ireland). The Policy Studies Institute has estimated[13] that other types of non-national museum have a combined expenditure of £42m, so that the whole museum sector is worth some £406m annually.

Nevertheless it is a fact that many – even most – museums face financial difficulties. This is partly a product of wider economic policy, chiefly of government failure to increase grant-in-aid to national museums in line with pay awards to public servants, and of restrictions on the amount local authorities are allowed to spend, and partly a reflection of the increasing demands being made by museums on their paymasters as standards rise and new facilities are opened. The result is, in the national museums, a widening funding gap between the museums' grant-in-aid and the money they need to fulfil their basic functions. Local authorities, many of which are faced on the one hand with what may seem an inadequate Standard Spending Assessment from the government, and on the other with the danger or risk of being charge-capped, sometimes find it hard to give priority to museums, especially when the alternative is having to cut social services or education budgets. There is no legal obligation on local authorities to provide a museum service. In this respect museums are unlike libraries. Elsewhere, many independent museums are financially weak and in danger of closure, and have been urged in a recent report commissioned by the Association of Independent Museums[14] to consider establishing management networks and consortia.

The independent museum sector led the way in the early 1970s by developing the practice of plural funding, by charging for admission of necessity, developing retail activities to generate income, seeking business sponsorship, and introducing marketing techniques. In a few instances collection care suffered in consequence, although most independent museums are well aware of the dangers of this. Fortunately, relatively few of them have very large collections and the sort of responsibilities in that regard faced by most publicly funded museums, after 100 years or so of acquisition/accretion. Most independent museums started relatively recently with fairly closely defined terms of reference for collecting. However, by the 1980s publicly funded museums had been forced to follow down the road of plural funding and improved marketing.

Admission Charges

Most people working in UK museums would instinctively prefer to see no charge made for admission. They see a charge deterring the poor, the casual and the repeat visitor, and fundamentally contradicting the museum's founding educational purpose. They see it as a breach of faith with past donors and as a disincentive to future donors. They point to the initial 40% or higher fall in attendances and increased cost per visitor experienced by almost every museum that has introduced charges, and to the likely fall in trading revenue from the museum shop and catering that results from charging.

Others in museums have, despite these arguments, become convinced that charging is not simply unavoidable in harsh economic terms, but is actually appropriate and right in principle. They argue that a system of concessions can cater for young, poor, old, local and regular visitors; that the interests of past and future donors can be safeguarded; that the initial fall in attendance is commonly checked and reversed after about three years; that charges enable a museum to improve its visitor-facilities (shop, cafeteria, lavatories etc), and thus to increase its trading revenue; and finally that an admission charge obliges a museum to think in value-for-money terms, and thus to improve its service to the public.

Both these approaches are valid. Neither has a monopoly of virtue. Each combines principle with practice. Both views are strongly held, and the debate continues. The MGC's own view, which it shares with the Museums Association, is that a funding authority should not put pressure on a museum to introduce charges in order to meet its basic running costs; given this, the decision to charge or not is one for an individual museum to make; but, if a charge is made, the revenue raised should be retained by the museum and separately shown in the accounts, and there should be appropriate concessions and the equivalent of one free day a week.

Whatever one's personal view, the fact is that whereas until 1984 entry to the main building of all national museums had been free, now eight of the nineteen charge. It is clear that in most instances the decision to do so was taken with regret and influenced by an insufficient grant from the government department concerned. Charging has long been acceptable for special exhibitions and at certain specialised branch museums. Three quarters of the national museums now regularly charge for admission to some or all of their buildings or branches. The trend seems set to continue.

Corporate Planning and Marketing

If the 1980s saw museums taking a leap forwards into the new world of plural funding, they also saw museums starting to evolve corporate strategies and adopting a more positive approach to forward planning. The process of drawing up a corporate plan and revising it annually helps a museum to define and redefine its objectives, assess its achievements and formulate its requirements and relate them to projected funding. We have recently published guidance on this.[15] In many cases the discipline of preparing a plan has led museums to rethink their approach to marketing and to business sponsorship.

Most museums have come new to marketing, and even now only about 40 employ a full-time marketing officer. But there is plenty of talent in the outside world and it is becoming easier for museums to obtain basic marketing advice and training. We have recently published the results of a limited programme of grant-aid and advice on this subject, and we welcome the prospect of more museums adopting a market-oriented approach. But far more needs to be done, and a much greater investment is needed by museums and by the Government.

Business sponsorship is well-established as a means by which commercial firms undertake, in return for appropriate advertising exposure, to finance or underwrite a museum project – most commonly a temporary exhibition, but also other events and publications. Museums are well aware that even in good times sponsorship deals can be struck only for highly visible activities, and are unlikely to cover routine expenditure. For a number of reasons museums have never been as successful in attracting sponsorship as other art forms and their search has been made harder by the cutback in corporate promotion that has accompanied the recession. And although the number of companies involved in arts sponsorship has continued to rise, the number of arts and museum organisations seeking such partnerships is probably rising even faster.

Donations and Voluntary Help

The introduction of gift-aid in 1990, which now allows single donations to museums of £400 or more to be offset against tax, provided a rather more flexible and attractive alternative to deeds of covenant, although there is little evidence that museums have benefited. Where museums have always been particularly successful is in the use they make of voluntary effort.

A large proportion of the 1100 independent museums rely heavily on the use of volunteers. Many are staffed entirely by this means, others rely on them for reception and shop duties or for conservation and restoration work. The contribution made by such volunteers is remarkable and commendable, as is that of the 150,000 who – usually through one of the 200 Friends' organisations – help in various ways in the running of many larger museums, even nationals. This unpaid input also extends to a senior level. In Britain the members of museum governing bodies, whether they are Trustees appointed by government for the nationals, local authority elected members, or Board members of independent museums, all serve on a voluntary basis.

When one also considers the extent to which museum collections (and indeed buildings) have been donated in the past, and how the members of the National Art Collections Fund continue to provide help today, and how museums raise money through voluntary contributions, it is clear that museums do rely very considerably on the goodwill of a large sector of their supporters. But in many instances this community is an ageing one. The director of a leading independent museum recently commented that he feared the onset of winter, not for its effect on his visitor numbers but because a sudden cold snap could easily wipe out a couple of his Trustees! Younger people with family and career commitments face many other demands on their spare time. One of the challenges now facing museums, particularly in the independent sector, is to engage the active support of a new generation.

The Geffrye Museum's education service has worked hard to reach across social and cultural barriers, to bring the museum's users into close contact with historical objects. The Museum is playing an increasingly significant role in the life of Hackney, a poor East London borough which is home to Bangladeshi, Chinese and other minority communities. Here two children discuss their project with Director David Dewing. For many this museum is an oasis in a bleak urban landscape, and an excellent example of the way in which museums, in serving their community, can act as a catalyst for urban regeneration.

The Future and some Recommendations 8

The Nation's Heritage

The collections contained in our museums and galleries are some of the finest in the world and it is the role of museums to ensure they are properly cared for on behalf of the nation, and that they are understood and enjoyed. Museums should meet agreed standards and should be operated on a basis that does not put their collections at risk. The registration scheme sets minimum standards and has ensured that museums have appropriate constitutional frameworks, precisely defined collecting policies, and meet basic standards of collection care. It also provides the basic eligibility criteria for grant aid from the MGC and from many other funding bodies. **All museums should aim to achieve full registration status.**

Over two-thirds of museums applying for registration have used the occasion to reconsider and set out clearly their collecting policy. This consideration is an essential first step towards rationalising collections and developing national, regional and sub-regional collecting agreements. Collecting policies should maximise the opportunities for collaboration with other museums. During the last few years collection surveys have been undertaken in some parts of the country and in some subject areas to find out where collections are, what is in them and in what condition they are being held. This process now needs to be completed in order to make strategic decisions about the long-term care and distribution of collections. All museums should aim to meet the care of collections standards now being developed. But if they are to meet these standards and undertake the necessary surveys, additional funding will be needed. **Further investment is also urgently needed to clear backlogs in documentation and achieve adequate storage conditions.** The MGC and the Area Museum Councils have long sought significant increases in their budgets so that effective incentives can be offered to museums and partnerships forged with local authorities and the other sources of museum funding. Museums also need help so that they may continue to acquire material for their collections. **The purchase grants for national museums and the local purchase funds and the National Heritage Memorial Fund should be increased; tax relief be allowed for gifts in kind to museums; and the tax incentive or douceur when items are offered under the acceptance in lieu procedures should be increased from 25% to 50%.** And we urge the Government to implement the recommendations of its own Export Reviewing Committee on how the procedures for export control may be improved without resorting to banning the export of important items. Our control system is universally admired but has been starved of cash. The number of heritage items coming into the saleroom or threatened with export seems likely to increase and there are worrying signs that the vendors will increasingly include semi-public bodies as well as private owners.

Our concern for collections is not confined to their acquisition and physical care. They must be interpreted and displayed, which means they must be understood and be the subject of research and scholarship. We are concerned that scholarship is increasingly perceived as under threat. **All museums should state and monitor in their corporate plans and annual reports the intellectual standards at which they are aiming.** We recommend furthermore that **larger museums should introduce peer group review to help in the mutual assessment of this aspect of their work.**

Museum Buildings

In the last few years there has been a welcome recognition of the fact that the nation's stock of arts buildings is in urgent need of repair and improvement. The Government has already pledged itself to restore the national museums by the end of the century and has increased greatly its funding for this purpose. But a recent consultant's report for the Government demonstrated that still more needs to be done: the costs for the twelve DNH funded national museums alone have been tentatively put at £1 billion. A large proportion of the non-national museums also need further investment in their buildings, many of which are also listed and of considerable importance locally. We shall undertake a survey to quantify these needs more precisely, but they are likely to amount to a further £1 billion to restore existing buildings and to undertake important developments that will help safeguard the collections they contain. These figures take no account of any proposals for new museums, which would have to be looked at very carefully.

A National Lottery

The Government's White Paper on the National Lottery and subsequent Ministerial statements made it clear that the fabric of our museum buildings and the rescue of major heritage items will be high among the list of beneficiaries. We welcome this. Museums are distributed throughout the UK – there are on average four in each parliamentary constituency – and appeal to residents and tourists alike. In recent years they have done much to help themselves and have demonstrated that they can usually more than match any money provided by government or through such schemes as the Museum Improvement Fund. Unfortunately, non art museums have been declared to be largely outside the terms of reference of the Sports and Arts Foundation, which has provided grants of £500,000 for other arts buildings. **Museums and galleries should be a separate and major category of beneficiary of the National Lottery for contributions towards the cost of housing their collections and of acquiring major heritage items. In addition endowment funds should be set up for certain museums with collections of national significance not directly supported by government or by local authorities.** It is in the taxpayer's interest that such museums should maintain their independent status, and in many instances a relatively small amount of guaranteed income would help them to stay afloat financially and meet appropriate standards of collection care. Endowments should be only offered on a very selective basis to half a dozen museums each year. But over a ten year programme most of the priority cases would have been dealt with. This would accord with the Government's expressed intention of using the proceeds of the National Lottery to protect and safeguard our heritage, much of which is portable and in the custody of museums.

People

In recent years museums have demonstrated a greater awareness of the need to cater more for the needs of their visitors and to market themselves better. But much remains to be done and incentives are needed to help in extending audiences to take account of the cultural diversity of the population and of the needs of those with disabilities. The **educational role and potential of museums should be recognised by the Government, with special funding for the MGC and AMCs.** One of the best ways of increasing access and winning new audiences is through travelling exhibitions, particularly with those that draw on material from the national collections. The Civil War exhibition, featuring material from the Tower Armouries and sponsored by "The Times" and funded by the MGC, has been breaking box office records as it travels around the country. Museums are keen to do more if the money can be found.

Much of what needs to be done to improve museums hinges on improved training. The Museum Training Institute requires the full financial support of government and the participation of all sectors of the museum community in its vital work of standard setting, influencing providers of training, and increasing employers' awareness that training is not a luxury but an essential investment. **All museums should produce staff training policies and set aside at least 2% of their staffing budgets for training.** For far too long too many museums have been kept in the doldrums by those responsible for running them. Early retirement has been used to solve such problems, but is no substitute for proper training and increased opportunities for career progression. There is also a need for greater uniformity in pay and grading structures for people doing similar work in similar museums under different funding authorities. Some Keeper posts in university museums are paid a half of what would be considered appropriate in a national museum for dealing with collections of equal size and importance.

The advent of a Single European Market after 1992 has alerted the UK museum community to the need to improve linguistic abilities among staff. **More money needs to be made available to help museum staff to travel**

abroad and broaden their experience. In general there is little co-operation at working level within Europe, and hardly any exchanges of staff such as one might expect to see between Community partners.

The European dimension is one of which the Museums Training Institute is, we know, well aware in its systematic approach to the establishment of standards of competence for all museum staff. The aim must be to develop a system of museum training in the UK which other countries, in Europe and elsewhere, will wish to emulate. **By the year 2000 there should be mutual recognition of professional qualifications.**

Another area in which the UK already leads is conservation. The conservation profession is a relatively new one all over the world. In the UK a strong tradition has developed, combining private conservators with those in the public sector, and the UK profession is well regarded in other European countries. In consequence it is well placed to take advantage of opportunities within Europe that may occur after 1992. The MGC's Conservation Unit has taken the lead in pursuing this approach and was instrumental last year in setting up ECCO, the European Confederation of Conservator-Restorers Organisations.

Museum Growth – and Decline

Inevitably, in a time of economic recession, the museum world must be especially concerned to ensure that scarce resources are not squandered on ill-conceived museum projects that have little prospect of survival. There is nothing to stop anyone in this country from opening a museum, but 2,500 museums is probably too many. We need fewer and better, not more. **Anyone contemplating starting a museum must seek advice beforehand, and consider the annual running costs** once the capital cost has been met and the initial enthusiasm of those responsible has perhaps waned. The local AMC will be able to advise on the prospects of the museum being registered (or provisionally registered). Unless it is so registered, the museum will not attract grants from the AMC, the MGC or many other sources of funding.

We are concerned about the standards museums offer to the public and whether there is a sufficient audience or financial resource to sustain the recent growth in numbers. The years ahead will undoubtedly see more mergers and rationalisations, and an increase in the number of closures. The MGC is considering, with other organisations, how best to evolve a code of practice for dealing with museum closures, with the object of saving the museum's collections and where possible transferring them to a suitable alternative. Collections must be safeguarded in the event of a closure. **Reform of charity law is urgently needed to give better legal protection to museum collections** in such circumstances. At present a charity may be forced to sell the very material it was set up to protect, and the laws which oblige charity trustees to obtain the highest possible price for their 'assets' in the event of a sale can easily prevent transfer to another museum. Together with the Museums Association, we are also investigating the legal status of local authority collections and it is likely that this will need to be clarified.

Towards a National Policy for Museums

The creation of the new Department of National Heritage, headed by a Secretary of State, provides the opportunity to formulate a Government policy on museums. Even without a formal policy the DNH, as lead Department for museums, should be able to influence the actions of other Departments with museum responsibilities, to ensure that all Departments are made aware of the effects of proposed policies on museums, and help to minimise differences between departments on policy issues (*eg* rules on the ownership of collections, the treatment of earned income and the provision of funds for capital development). Already the DNH and the Ministry of Defence are considering future arrangements for supporting the armed service museums, recognising that their collections form an important part of the national heritage. An even more urgent and difficult problem needs to be addressed: **the Government should review the future funding arrangements for the 300 university museums and collections.** The changes in the way in which the universities are financed and the imminent replacement of the Universities Funding Council present an ideal opportunity to grasp this nettle.

Any national policy for museums must clearly take full account of the differing needs, traditions and aspirations of parts of the UK including local

In bringing together children from both sides of the sectarian divide in Northern Ireland, the Ulster Folk & Transport Museum's Education for Mutual Understanding (EMU) programme is helping prepare the ground for a more peaceful future in the Province. Among the EMU programme activities at the Museum's Drumnahunshin Farmhouse site children can learn at first hand about traditional ways of doing the household chores.

communities, and reflect the differing needs of the subject areas covered. Its formulation will be helped by the availability soon of better statistics about museums. We do not believe it is practicable or desirable for museum development to be centrally planned, still less centrally controlled, and we could not endorse any form of national plan (beyond adherence to agreed national standards) with which local interests would have to conform. Nor do we advocate legislation requiring all local authorities to provide and maintain museums, for we do not believe this is practicable. But **each local authority should adopt a museums policy to ensure an appropriate level of museum provision in its area,** taking account of existing museums of all types in the vicinity. We also **recommend that the Government include and set out realistic components for museums in the Standard Spending Assessment figures given to local authorities.** We see the role of local authorities as central to the support of all types of non-national museums in the next few years. More can undoubtedly be done in partnership with other agencies and the private sector, and to take advantage of such schemes as City Challenge funding. The needs of museums will have to be taken into account when the future structure of local government is being considered. Much has been achieved by many of the County Councils in England; the experience of joint committees of District Councils running museums has not always been happy. The combination of ill-conceived boundary changes and continued financial pressures threatens to undo much of what local authorities have achieved over the last twenty years.

In general we would like to see greater collaboration between museums at all levels. Over many years the MGC and AMCs have encouraged museums to work together to pool resources and expertise, and many local authorities now employ qualified museum staff to provide pastoral care for small volunteer-run museums. Indeed such museums need access to a professional curatorial adviser in order to be registered. A framework of Countywide Consultative Committees or Regional Forums already exists in much of Britain to encourage such things as complementary collecting policies, shared support services and co-operation on travelling exhibitions. And we strongly support the proposal advocated in the report commissioned for AIM in 1990:[13] that neighbouring museums of all sorts (and even some non-museums) should develop functional networks, or consortia, with a focus on management services. Whatever form interdependence takes – pastoral care, co-operation or networking – museums will need more of it during the 1990s if they are to survive and improve their service to the public.

The AMCs have a central role to play in this, but they are not as well known as they deserve to be. Increasingly they work in close conjunction with other regional bodies and with local authorities. They are essential partners to the MGC in our own work and are ideally placed to do a great deal more through advice, providing shared services and, most importantly, backing up that advice with the ability to offer realistic levels of funding. But a total of £3.5m divided between ten AMCs is not a realistic amount and restricts their ability to fulfil their potential. **Funding for the AMCs should be doubled in real terms,** and we regard this as one of our highest priorities.

Conclusion

We fully appreciate that more money at this time will be hard to come by, and we have indicated a number of ways in which, without significant extra funds, museums can help themselves and improve the service they provide for the public. We are looking for closer collaboration and interdependence, readiness to consider rationalising collections, better corporate planning, and co-operation in developing and raising standards. We believe the museum community has both the will and the capacity to meet the challenges it will face between now and the end of the century.

The MGC will continue to work closely with the museum community, with the AMCs, the Museums Association and the Association of Independent Museums and other museum bodies, and with the Government Departments and agencies concerned in raising intellectual and care-of-collection standards in museums and thus improving the service they provide to the public.

The future for museums is wide open, not only in this country but in Europe as a whole. The public demand has never been higher. The challenges and opportunities have never been greater; museums can meet the challenges; they need to be helped to grasp the opportunities.

Museums are increasingly aware of the importance of making their displays accessible to as wide an audience as possible. At the National Waterways Museum a young wheelchair user tries out a pulley device demonstrating different forms of lifting cargo.

And now read on . . .

This list of published sources referred to in the text also serves as a reading list for those who wish to find out more. A complete list of MGC publications is available from our Information Officer.

1 British Tourist Authority, *UK Tourism Survey,* 1990, British Tourist Authority, London.

2 Research Surveys of Great Britain, *Arts and Cultural Activities in Great Britain* (Omnibus Survey), 1991, Arts Council of Great Britain.

3 Museums & Galleries Commission, *Museum Professional Training and Career Structure,* 1987, HMSO, London.

4 Museums & Galleries Commission, *Museums and Galleries Commission Annual Report 1989–90,* 1990, HMSO, London.

5 Thompson, J. M. A. (ed), *Manual of Curatorship: A Guide to Museum Practice,* 1984 (1st edition), Butterworths/The Museums Association, London.

6 Lord, Barry, Dexter Lord, Gail and Nicks, John, *The Cost of Collecting: Collection Management in the UK Museums,* 1989.

7 Public Accounts Committee, 'The Management of the Collections of the English National Museums and Galleries 1987–88', *First Report, 1989–90,* 1989, National Audit Office, London.

8 The Audit Commission, *The Road to Wigan Pier? Managing Local Authority Museums and Art Galleries,* 1991, HMSO, London.

9 London Museums Service and London Museums Consultative Committee, *"Dingy places with different kinds of bits": an attitude survey of London Museums amongst non-visitors,* 1991, London Museums Service/London Consultative Committee, London.

10 Myerscough, John, *The Economic Importance of the Arts in Britain,* 1988, Policy Studies Institute, London.

11 Museums & Galleries Commission, *The National Museums,* 1987, HMSO, London.

12 Museums & Galleries Commission, *Local Authorities and Museums,* 1991, HMSO, London.

13 *Cultural Trends Number 14: Museum Finances,* 1992, Policy Studies Institute.

14 Middleton, Victor, T. C., *New Visions for Independent Museums in the UK,* 1990, Association of Independent Museums.

15 Ambrose, Timothy and Runyard, Sue (eds), *The Forward Planning Handbook,* 1991, Routledge.

'All aboard!' as a 1925 Gateshead & District tram takes visitors along the half-mile route between the Entrance Building and the Town at the North of England Open Air Museum in Beamish near Durham. The most well-known of Beamish's displays is the Edwardian Town Street, complete with shops, pub and dwelling houses, which are brought to life by demonstrators. For many of its half-million annual visitors Beamish is a trip down memory lane, whilst for others it provides a fascinating and historically authentic glimpse into their parents' and grandparents' lives.